Why Did I Remain in the Garden?

Poems and Short Prose

George Wylie

PSI

Poetry
Society of
Indiana

George acknowledges Rita for her great support and proofreading, Dennis White for his steadfast mentoring, Michael Amidei for his example and encouragement, my brother Kenneth Wylie who stands as my symbol of writing quality, and the wonderful help from poet/author Jenny Kalahar on this book.

The photos are the creation of the author, including the covers.

Is There an App for Goodbye?

I lost some people last year
Am not ready to ask why
The answers aren't abundantly clear
Is there an app for goodbye?

They left a hole in my life
Technology doesn't tell me why
At least they're gone from this strife, but
Is there an app for goodbye?

When they're stopped before their time
And had not yet accessed their sky
And simple faith does not define
Is there an app for goodbye?

There is Gold in Grandmothers

There is gold in grandmothers
They hold the chalice of a granddaughter's trust
The bond is rarely broken throughout life
They will dote on each other forever
... even when one or the other is gone.

Why Did I Remain in the Garden?

I remained there because it was my wish to stay
until the hibiscus was done stretching its petals
Until the hummingbird was sated in her whirr for the nectar.
I did not depart because a green bottle fly
was still aboard a thistle blossom

Because the breeze was making a red poppy
seem to dance beyond the wisteria.
Because a red-winged blackbird was bothering
a red squirrel by the fence,
and because a gladiola was about to be born,
midwifed by two bees.
So I stayed to finish my coffee.
To see if the goldfinches would find the tiny seeds.

Will the brown bee bury its head in the moist red lily
or the tall cosmos?
Would the night rain that kisses the roses
keep them shy until after dawn?
Would it keep the adolescent blossoms
from bluntly charging at the sky?
Would it keep the honeybees from the red coneflower's
salacious solicitations?

On mornings, I'd find small bumblebees in the cosmos blossoms,
still and apparently dead,
until I read that they often sleep overnight within the bold petals…
too weary at dusk are they, the book said,
to return to the distant hive.
They just do sleepovers among the wanton blooms
and commence feeding at dawn.

There is room at my inn for these little lifespans—
the garden gate is open.
Nary a flower, bird, or butterfly
is cast away whilst I sit in the garden
Do the goldfinches and wrens know I love them,
that I won't harm them?
My vow is my feeding them, my testament is growing them
new havens and hideaways

I stayed in the garden to see the florid harvest,
to know that nature is not indifferent,
but instead it calls the flowers to me, and me to them.
There is wild nature and stern nature,
but also there is my garden nature,
which lures me to them, and perhaps, warms them to me.

I don't just come to the lilacs, the poppies,
the alyssum, the honeysuckles.
They come to me, and I'll stay there as long as they wish
For I'm a wallflower and I just don't want to miss the dance.
So that is why I'll stay. At least until the bumblebees go to bed.

Loose Lips

A normal man had lessons learned
But me; my punishments I earned
Advice from others I have spurned

You see I always talk too much
When even not in a real clutch
I mutter such and such and such

The muscle that has lost my grip
is the one that closes down my lips
and we all know loose lips sink ships

I give myself my biggest dangers
I'm known to bother even strangers
So please send me a verbal ranger

Hello, it's me and I will talk
So you'd best not delay your walk
Else fit me with a lip padlock.

Hurried Words at the Grave

Emptied, we stood at his last breath.
Harried, unshaven, we'd hurried
to beat the last chime of his life.

Road weary and rumpled, we had but little notice
No time, no plans, no edited drafts.
For this most vital time we'd not practiced.

No careful resume of his life was done
Each of us having a need to show our caring
And the kind of homage he deeply deserved

And to glean out from all the things he'd done.
This man was better by far than all the rest.
We thought there'd be more years before he cast away

How could our quickly conjured words serve a superior man?
No doubt he'd be embarrassed by our palsied eulogies
He was leaving while we fabricated plastic praises

And he probably planned it that way.

Water

I love water
I drink water
I stare at water
I bathe in water
I have lived on water
I often go towards water
On water   I've had boats
I ride my bike towards water
I photograph water, because it is water
My ancestors were water people in Scotland, maybe
Everything looks better upon the water
I eat fresh fish from the water
Pollution is ruining the water
We're running out of water
Fish often poop in water
Fish have sex in water
life depends on water
Water equals life
I am water
Water

The Things He Never Saw

So many things have come to pass
since he died in eighty-nine.
Some bad, some good, those things he missed,
I'm choosing now the fine.
The things my father never saw
have fueled my pen this time.

A man of index cards and lists.
A math and physics teacher.
A natural for spreadsheets,
he'd have cherished a computer
to quickly Google-up a fact
would endear him to the cursor.

But deep among the things he missed,
like grandkids graduating,
are his legacy of humans,
with children's eyes adoring.
Like babies on his friendly lap
and the lilt of children singing

But the news I'd like to have Dad hear,
Which would meet with his approval,
is that we progeny have his gentility,
and we love words, especially verbal.
So, if we did indeed absorb his thirst for love and learning
… does that not prove what we suspect: our parents are immortal?

Night Winds

Heard through doors and windowsills,
these night winds have brought their chills

A bit of song, a trace of danger,
at times a friend, at times a stranger.

They bear foreboding; carry rain.
Prattle up my windowpane.

I venture out for confirmation
And only see leaf litteration.

Back to my chair, my book is there.
Night winds are common, no need to care.

But night winds prove my jurisdiction
is just a part of my own fiction.

Shutters shook and branches fell.
The winds which came know me too well.

Just Another Lake Sunset

Hand-painted clouds draw down the day
and beckon the ducks to shore
as the horizon straightens to a gilded edge.

The water's front line of foam and sand
is diminished to smallness as the light retreats
and the bravado of the day's water becomes a sunset's blush.

The blued, then pearled, then purpled clouds
begin the wisp of somber departure.
The orange sun pulls them down like a nightshade.

A tiny pajamad child taps my shoulder
complaining he can't yet sleep.
I draw him under my warm wool jacket – we hush and we watch

The small waves pull up their sheets
over the chin of the beach
and await the darkness.

To abandon a sunset just as it sets
is a mistake in love and judgement.
For the glory after the red orb leaves - is fully half the show.

An old cork bobber turns up on the shore
as the languid scent of drying sand
activates my childhood memories.

The beached grains of sand, retired from their moving duty
now dry themselves into the small footprints of shore birds,
their indentations now stay intact, unwashed.

The overhanging oak leaves are darkened and silhouetted
as the background of sky turns its power over to the stars
and a heron stops in with a leg up on its shallow prey

The quietude, the flatness of it all
as a waxing moon greets the oncoming Venus
while a loon announces its pure magic with a tremolo.

Now full nightness has enveloped the shore.
The line between water and sky is gone.
My nature lesson tween man and boy, is now complete
… and the child is full asleep.

Did I Blister Our Best Chances?

Did I drop the verbals hard
Did I blast you with my bitters
Did I scour out your heart
Did I tangle your heart's innards?

Would I scar what makes you thee
Would I damn the future perfect
Would I hurt the us-ness of we
Would I scourge what we reflect?

Might I find here some repeal
Might I bandage some arrears
Might you seek a place to heal
Might you consider the good years?

Can we gather up the fixings
Can we make a meal from those
Can we build us up more tidings
Can we … what do you suppose?

A Hole in the Woods

There is always a hole in the woods, you know
A hole where the timid don't dare
But to pass through that hole in the woods, you go
to a place that can go anywhere.

I Could But Dream

She shifted her desk a bit, perchance, I fantasized, to see me better
My brain was ginning up facts without substance.
There, did she look at me?
She grinned at the teacher, rendering him, I assumed, into a rapture
Did she love anyone, hate anyone, care about anything?

How in the world could any man not be in love with her?
At my fifteen years of nuclear hormonal bombardment,
I could but dream
The long legs crossed as her feet moved just enough to shake the laces
Parts of me stirred. Was this a dream from the treasures of sunbeams?

Some of her yellow hair fell over her green eyes, adding a mystery
Who was she peeking at from under that crown of gold?
She often put a pencil in her mouth and twisted it a bit in an out
I could see the fine hairs on her arms as she wrote with her left hand.

Each day she grew more beautiful, maturing as I watched her
I must hurry or she'd fly into someone else's pulsing arms
How could I accelerate my coolness to the point she noticed?
Would I appear more seductive if I ignored her, or if I stared at her?

She had a low husky voice and answered
the teacher's questions with a smile.
He accepted her answers gladly…. even when she was wrong
Had the spirits lofted her into my classroom like a grand gilded gift?
Even if she probably didn't even know my name?

One day she smiled at me in the hallway
 and I almost tripped over my feet.
I decided to ask her to the Autumn Hop.
The fear of my decision suspended all else
I was consumed with the thought of dancing with her,
 could I control my eagerness?
I resolved to ask her the next day.

I would not chicken out. I WOULD do it!

What? She was not in class the next day. She never missed class.
And the next day too.
I approached a girl who knew her and inquired.
"Oh, Marlene? She moved ...
... went to live with her father in Wisconsin. I knew you'd ask.
I've been watching you watch her all the time. You are pretty pathetic. "

"Did she ever mention me?"
"No. She didn't even know your name.
By the way, who are you asking to the dance?"
"You."

New Town, New Walks

I had to tread lightly where the nervous dogs lie sleeping
where the garbage is spilled onto the walkway
where the guy who grows great dahlias lives
where the parents loudly curse their kids.
Just moved here and wanted to know where the friendly people are.
To find that poorer streets have more shade trees
and the kids are allowed to play outside,
allowed to play alone in puddles or dirt
where the bicycles are hand-me-downs,
tossed down on their sides without guilt.
I seemed to sense when people are out of town
but have disguised their houses to look inhabited.
And when all the windows in a house are closed and blinded
against what must be perceived as a cruel world.
Should I knock at their door and with a big grin,
explain community to them?
No, valuing my life, I hurried on.
An older nicely-dressed woman with maybe a German accent
spoke to me once
as I happened by and surprised her while she picked trash
from an acrid dumpster.
Startled, she wiped her hands with a clean towel
and tried vainly to explain.
"I don't have much, you know.
The people over there are usually mean to me."
She pointed at a house.
"Well, Good luck," I said, my words more empty than hers.
The most heroic thing I could summon
was to glare directly at that house.
I had to know how distant a train is to activate
the clanging bell and to stop me.
And standing there returned me to my childhood practice
of counting rail cars.
I also learned that when walking by the river on a foggy morning,
a freighter's horn can almost soil your clothing

And where rivers and train tracks prevail,
the streets are indecisive and disjointed.
And where they've stripped off all trees to make redundant new houses.
I learned where the best surviving front porches are
And where the hydrangeas and hibiscus grow.
Could I judge a homeowner by their gardening skills
Or judge a man by his truck, or a kid by his lowered pants?
Might I judge if an ancient oak was felled
to make room for a trampoline?
But I am the one walking by. I am the observer.
No one asked me to stroll by.
So a better question is, might they all be judging me?
Hoping not, I hurried on.
The walks in my new town, especially at morning,
are my textbook, my footing.
What is this town's personality?
The slowness of walking lets me focus and deduce,
while on my bike, it is a bit too fast
And rushing along in my car, I am hopelessly sterilized and unseeing.
For me it is to walk and put my feet where my mouth is,
even if they are often in it.
In a summer whose heat and humidity is unforgiving
the walks are freshening my old man's senses
My town is coming alive, step by step, block by block, week by week,
Like watching an old talkie movie getting slowly colorized with sound.
The best walk is a wander, with no goals in view
The best view is yonder, not simply a step or two
Go where your nose and eyes take you, like kids do
Go for a walk like dogs do.

Running Up Against

He ran up against the walls of manners
Ran up against expediency
He pushed against the pops of culture
And fought the fads of currency

He had no urge to patronize
Or dote on crying babies
Disdained the need for handshakes
And never winked at ladies

He could not, would not ride a fence
He danced around the rules
His courtesies were limited
And he could not suffer fools

And as his days dimmed towards the sun
He could not gather close his kin
And he spent his farewells scowling out
to a world ... not looking in.

Water Dances on the Big Lake

We spent many years at the big lake,
watched closely by a huge aggressive load of sky,
which could be fickle as a fly, then angry as a wild boar,
and then welcoming as a rose arbor.

We perched there on the shore for two decades.
Large unblinking windows aimed at the water.
We gathered sunsets in a basket and raindrops in our hats,
Had our breakfasts on the dock and sunburned beer in a boat.

And of course, wondrous sunsets of cerulean,
presenting first with purple clouds
then growing like a Phoenix, with brushed on gold
and orange and hues of peace,
and climaxing like a slow-motion DeMille showcase,
backed by a soundtrack of geese and loons …
 and the sadness of departure.

After sunsets we watched the firepit embers weave their way
to the approaching Venus
and witnessed the purple-black curtain of hesitant stars
tenting slowly over us.
With fireflies and marshmallows in our hair
we watched Ursa Major grow
And heard the quiet murmur of trolling night fishermen.

The lights on the distant shore moved with the water edges
and urged a night breeze into a jiggling song.
And at dawn the bigger fish ventured near the dock.
If you sat still on the dock
peering down through the water at the yellow sand,
you would see their minnow-seeking waltz shadow its way
over the sand's geometric grooves.

Local legend says Ojibwa families loved this west-facing shore

where steady breezes
kept mosquitos at bay,
and the Old Saginaw Indian trail was but yards away.
Now, if you breathe in the lucid air,
close your eyes and take it back two hundred years:
It is morning and there are women wading towards the dropoff
with their fishing weirs,
while nearby their children splash water into the sun.

Bundles of Purity: Armloads of Trust

How can I not love the warmth of their little heads,
the power of their powerlessness, the lilt of their smiles,
the bright eyes that follow me, the total dependence,
and the way their tiny hand grips my fingers?

How can I not love the doll-like feet that jump about,
the urge to protect, to hug and savor,
and how they bring out the best and warmest of us?
How can I not love this bundle of purity, this armload of trust?
How do I know I'm worthy of such treasure?

Breaded Mozzarella Sticks

My friends were not the topmost kind.

They took me in only because we graded each other on a curve.

The Chesapeake & Ohio line ran through town near Ed Fortune's bar.

And we were always on the track's wrong side … no matter where we lived.

The good kids had cars with automatic transmissions and garages which actually held cars.

And their mothers put on makeup to buy groceries.

All their kids would go to college whether they wanted to or not.

And they had cottages on golden lakes where the sun always shone.

Their houses were brick and had venetian blinds, and someone else mowed their lawns.

And their parents spoke to them quietly, agreeably. I didn't think they even went to the bathroom, while our folks yelled a lot and the siblings might actually hit one another.

We got dirtier, we knew how to stalk a friend in the dark, and we were sure that was what made us cool

When our parents drove us to the dance, we asked them to drop us off a block away,

while the good kids glided shiningly up to the door and got out taking photos of each other.

Reverend Whiteship's daughter arrived, a prestigious sight to behold

But we knew her a bit better from over behind the pickle factory where she wasn't singing hymns.

The years drew on and they removed the train tracks.

Some of my friends and I—we had actually done quite well—occasionally blew back into town

to meet and drink beer together at Fortune's bar, which still stood.

But it had been "modernized" with barnwood and stuff to look much older than it actually was.

23

They now served breaded mozzarella sticks instead of pickled eggs from the big jar.

And, as was required in every local bar across the land,

a fat drunk slouched at the end of the bar, his eyes glued to the napkin.

The bartender said, "Oh that's Stace Barkman. He married Reverend Whiteship's daughter."

I asked "Didn't Stace's dad own half the town?

He answered, "Oh yes, but old man Barkman disowned Stace cause he's a drunk. And his wife left him." Stace heard his name spoken and looked over, then quickly looked away.

We changed the subject: "What are they doing with that great old train depot?" and the bartender said, "First some lady from up North turned it into a bible church called 'Della's Devotion Depot,' but it closed. So now it's gonna be a dollar store. People are pretty happy about that around here."

Word Questions

Could my words have enough power
to humble, to harm another?
What I write, could it heal or hinder or humor?
Might these words encourage or cause despair
Or tear someone else asunder?

Are my friends more favored by my silence than my words?
Does my rhetoric rise above others?
Should I deem it a quandary
that I might write better than I speak?
What if I am more candid on paper than by mouth?

We are defined by our actions, our speech, and our writing.
Which has more gravitas ... which is more binding?
The hypocrites lie with their words,
but the truth lies in their actions
and then they render the usual rationalization reaction.
Am I more apt to prevaricate on paper than in speech?

In front of our televisions we produce no actions
 but take in a million words.
From that, most of us produce almost nothing.
But we poetic pretenders try to regurgitate what we see
In words our peers may digest.
We must have a passion for language
or we turn away from our pens.

And when my words are inadequate, I resort to talking.
And those millions who are not able to act with words,
might just resort to swords.

Icy Shards of Winter

The crusted winds of boldness
Assaulting down the lands
With penetrating crassness
Red frosted cheeks and hands

The hurried clouds that parent
the blistered icy shards
The chilling unrepentant
With arctic disregards

I knocked upon your portal
Bid you to join my walk
But soon your hands were brittle
You could but barely talk

We hustled back accordingly
Our fortitude we shed
Tis better to be timid warm
Than very bravely dead

A love that thaws a frozen heart
Still falls to quell this season
I've never seen a poem smart
Enough to kill this freezin'

A Child's Dream Candle

I lit a candle with great care
And threw the candle in the air
Through wind it wavered just a bit
But holding all my dreams, stayed lit

And now I follow it each day
For me it always leads the way
And when it flickers in a storm
I send more hope to keep it warm.

The only time it will get dim
Is when I weaken from within
Just look, it hovers every hour
It gets its strength from my willpower.

Dawn Ripples

The first ripples come in just after dawn.
They touch the shore and crawl up to awaken the oaks.
The grass begins to sway and mutter
and two blue jays launch a morning chat.

The boat, newly re-christened by dawn,
edges leeward from its anchor.
The early breeze straightens a flag
as the lung-cleansing air overtakes the night.

The oak-floored and venerable cottage, inside and out
shows its class, its wear, and its seasoned crust,
all windows pointing outward, it announces its path through time
and with the children who splashed and dreamed here.

Almost a century of caretaking the lake,
this quaint place is a woodened and shuttered scrapbook of time,
of family and gentility, of old black and white photos
and faded board games
and of pushing away the city … and opening an old book.

Of dusty elk antlers and framed embroidery
Of creaky floors and wooden scrapbooks
that remember who trod here
Of a huge attic room, beds separated by hanging quilts
Of curtained cupboards and a well-stared-at fireplace

The lake and the cottage are the core
of what brings warm souls back each year,
back into the flooding memories as they enter.
So please sit with me on a lakeside Adirondack chair
and drink the coffee,
and watch the venerable and seductive first ripples of dawn.

The Rains of My Nights

The rains of my life have been kind,
and I treasure their acquaintances.
Rains to me have hue, they have a scent and a voice.
They clasp on me in different ways.
Brings back youthful nights when camping
and the rain pattering chopsticks on my canopy.
And serving up a rim of canvas security,
tucked in my bag with big brothers nearby.
I could haven't felt more safe and familial.
Across the decades of my life the rains have always helped me sleep.
And think.
In bigger tents with family and smaller tents with lovers
We looked for spots the rains come in and plug them with a laugh
If we were tired the rain was our guardian,
an excuse to move in and listen.
We sipped warm beer and dozed off
to the dimming chuckle of some old joke.
Escaping the flaps only to pee,
we returned to shake wet shirts at our companions.
Raising the boys, I taught them the joy of rain
and they learned to run into the splashes
To plunge into the warm torrent, worry not about dry clothing,
try to look up into rain without blinking.
And we learned to love the thunder and rumble. We added a skylight
in the family room just to see the dancing of drops on the glass. Both
boys have passed their love of rain and thunder onto their progeny.
We grew a family that rains well.
Now in my later more quiet years I haven't lost my love for rain, the
skittery dance of marching water.
The metal awnings add a vocal drumbeat to a rainy night and grow
the volume of a timid rain.
The tintinnabulation of the drops. (Sorry.) As always, I open
windows to better smell the rain.
A summer rain brings a hesitant hors d'oeuvre, then a main course,
and then it tiptoes back into the trees.

The flowers get high on the rain and later, under the following sun, they smile back up with gratuity.

Most poets metaphorically link sun with happiness and rain with turbulence and endings.

I prefer to love them both, and I try to reward each of them in kind.

I go out to meet a sun and also to greet a rain.

A rain is Nature tapping at your window. You should tap back.

The Family Bungalow

The storm windows needed to be hung each fall,
the screens exiled to the cellar.
It was not an abundant bungalow but an able abode,
the lives of five children etched inside.
Clapboard siding that deserved regular paint
yet was rewarded but a few times
A too-small kitchen that emitted enough sustenance for seven,
and always smelled right

One bathroom for seven, the tyrant of all the rooms,
it dictated its own order and respect,
Processing its clients just quick enough each school day
for our hygiene and privacy
A small water heater sang which rationed our baths
and our timekeeper mother to guide it
Handmade area rugs dappled the worn creaking floors,
protecting its busy intersections

A house that rose early and darkened late,
it mapped our growth and nursed us on
Just enough garden for roses and some carrots
and a big dependable rhubarb mound
A box elder we often fell from but provided summer's shade.
A small garage where our heads hit hanging ladders,
bikes and cobwebs

A yard that fenced in Tony The Bouncing Dog,
who once ate the neighbor's pet red-tailed hawk
Where Dad poked at dandelions with a hand weeder
and hinted at getting our help
Where robins were so used to children,
they hopped about us like traffic cops
Where an overly-dramatic persecuted child could flop
onto the grass in life-ending agony

She was a somewhat demure mother
but could make appropriate declarations when needed.

Her motherly acts were present but only when summoned.
She was the hesitant matron.
Who knew we knew where she put the cookies,
her parenting was benign but lasting.
She never loved that house nor bragged about it
but did both those things about her children.

She died peacefully in that house almost forty years ago.
Her progeny are now spread across the world
but I've driven by the house a few times.
For me its presence brings no brass fanfare
but rather a distant call of Oh Johnny Boy or Taps.
There are family marks hidden about the place
and only we kids know where they are.

I don't have the nerve to ask myself in,
and they wouldn't know me.
But the house just might.

Don't Ask Me Why

Don't ask me why I can't sing a love song
Can't play the piano with you at my arm
Can't make you a queen or me a king
Can't escort you to exotic places under foreign stars

You chose to be with me, don't ask me why
You accepted my arms and my kisses
Crawled among my blankets and ate my breakfasts
Huddled under an archway in the cold rain
Laughed when I fell and kissed my bruises
Told fibs to your friends so you could be with me
Don't ask me why you made my mornings live
And my evenings too short. You were perfection.

So when I decided to walk…don't ask me why
Why, I must have cried more than you did
Why was I so reticent, so smug, so distracted
You deserved to know and I failed you, cheated you.

There was no other person, no other choice
No fears, no negatives, no reasons
Some angular or misguided decision loomed
And I took it and I walked away

Maybe you were too good, too precious to keep
Maybe I thought I'd somehow wreck you
Maybe I feared I'd lose you. Don't ask me why
Perhaps I was afraid of a great life.

So I left you crying in that room those many years ago
Without a reasonable warning or explanation for your tears
And with almost no more contact with you, I just hiked
Darn it. Damn it. Don't ask me why.

Things Had Changed

He had lived in the world of boundaries
where even the birds had rules
and in a workplace of order
where one didn't touch others' tools
He'd survived a suburban setting where
nonconformity was the walk of fools.

He had thrived in a sea of voices
all caught in the same ebbtide
submerged in a world of material things
he'd lined dollars up side by side
Had endured the codes of propriety
And had neighbored well, kept in stride

But now that all had changed
He had moved, downsized, retired.
he could now wait for sunrise to take coffee
and sidestep what before was required.
he could appreciate smiles and trees and bees
his whole world was getting re-wired.

The morning wind now washed his hair
by the sun now his breath was measured
He could doze among the birds and breeze
and read the books he'd treasured

But where had all the people gone?
Those things that gave him urgency
And gone with them the turn signals
whose directions gave him gravity
Perchance this newfound freedom had
devalued all his currency.

The Stream of My Youth

At no place did the little stream of my youth flow straight.
It curved and switched and dropped as if to despise order.
My older brothers told me that every drop in the creek
would end in the ocean,
so I tried to spot a drop to see how loyal towards its goal it ran
But so quickly it fled and rushed away;
I could only imagine where it now was.
For now, I could not prove their claim
and so had only to trust my heart.

At one place in the sun, the creek had washed its way
under a huge oak root.
So large was the root that it formed a circle we could sit on
and submerge our bare feet into the cool dark water.
And maybe stir the mix to prod our own drops on to the Atlantic.
Would the ocean know that my drop came from me?
And would my drop be accepted
in the ocean's vast mixing pot of stream drops?

The brothers also advised that we could not
touch the same drop of water twice
That a drop of water was like time passing
and it would never be there again
To prove them wrong I tried touching a drop
and then running a few steps downstream
And touching it again.
They said I could not prove I'd touched the same drop.
And that drops were like golden fish:
once touched they'd drop to the deep.

My twin brother and I often sat together
with our feet in that wet circle of nature.

Treating it as if it owned its own circle of sky above,
so clearly reflected below
And we enhanced our import by splashing our credentials
to kids in London or Spain.
But, back atop our real circle we wondered
what thing next might bump our feet,
always a cause of great shouts, of dread,
of leapings up until it was deduced
to be a twig, a snake, or something bad floated in
by a sneaky upstream brother.

Against our mother's strongest speeches, we swam in that creek
And draped our clothes on the tag alders
until they dried enough to deceive Mom
In that circle and its approaches, we learned about the sun,
the creatures, and life's currents.
On a perch on a root of a tree on the little creek
by a little town in the middle of Michigan,
we caught crawfish and frogs and shiners there, then sent them
with our ideas and hopes, to Casablanca,
to Venice, or to Hong Kong.

… and to this day, no creek has returned to us
and proved we were wrong.

The Goldfinch Lands Lightly

The goldfinch lands lightly
on the thin-stemmed coreopsis
The sweet petalled buffet
is worth the fragile entry.
"Be gentle with me" says the flower.

Small Town at Night—Reprise

In my father's car I drive into our small town at night
It is after midnight; the wind pushes some drizzle
around the cross street
In the cruiser, Percy drifts up the street,
hoping he'll see nothing wrong
Just two cars at the tavern, lonely like a dim beacon in the mist
Some friends whisk by in a car, their laughter loud.
The meat market is boarded up where Mr. Snate blew his head off
right by the ground beef and chicken hocks and Wonder bread.
He had been arraigned a day earlier for molesting a child.
Lo Neeley walks by without a sound, bent under his wet hat.
They say before he went off to fight in the Bulge,
he was a star student,
with a deep singing voice and a future. He came home different.
He rarely speaks. They give him little jobs, like cleaning up Mr.
Spate's brains in the market.
Now he passes by on his way to sleep in his car behind the
depot...where he will one day die of asphyxiation.
Under old streetlights the brick sidewalks are like dark gator backs.
Wet mirrored puddles are deeper where folks tread the most.
A bike, too worn to steal, leans against the scarred door
of a walkup apartment
Percy slows to pass me, he knows me and waves,
his taillights waver away
I park by Mr. Braddock's little grocery.
He is rich now because he gave
Groceries to families during the decade-long Depression and kept a
tab. Very large tabs he called in when jobs came back, but the folks
didn't have the cash.
So they often paid him with land instead of money. Now he owns
lots of farmland.

Now a shiny new grocery has driven his store business to a trickle, but he doesn't care.

Some driver speeds up the street and squeals around the corner on Mill street. Percy lights up his cruiser and hurries by. He hates that he'll have to confront someone, maybe even stick them in the cell where the roof leaks and there is the dumb paperwork.

Mr. Schaupp the baker arrives with his key and goes in. He'll waft out the smell of bread and doughnuts from his oven vents all through the early morn.

When Percy can get one of the first offerings
and watch the town open up.

And I can drive down across the bridge's puddles to home and enter the house quietly, having done nothing of gainful worth.

Maybe tomorrow something will happen
And maybe it won't.

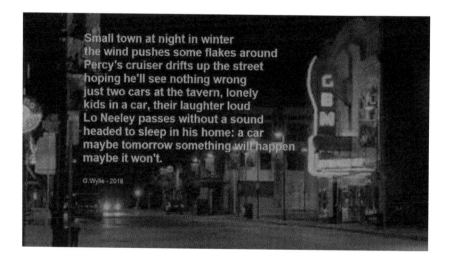

Small town at night in winter
the wind pushes some flakes around
Percy's cruiser drifts up the street
hoping he'll see nothing wrong
just two cars at the tavern, lonely
kids in a car, their laughter loud
Lo Neeley passes without a sound
headed to sleep in his home: a car
maybe tomorrow something will happen
maybe it won't.

G.Wylie - 2018

I Knew A Man Who Meant Me Dead

I knew a man who meant me dead
I knew not that, so did not dread
He seemed quite nice: a cheerful face
I had no sense I was his chase

We took to hills, a happy walk
Me seeking photos and leisure talk
He said he went to get away
From daily grinds and all the fray

He had a satchel, I had my pack
I saw his gun, he saw my snack
He claimed the gun was not a care
It was in case we met a bear

We lunched above a hardwood dale
I had a sandwich, he drank an ale
I wandered to the cliff and sun
I glanced and saw him get the gun

The only thing I thought to do
Was aim my camera and look through
And while he fired towards my head
I photographed him make me dead

But his shot missed, he rushed at me
I thrust my tripod at his knee
And way below he smashed upon the rocks
Oh my, I said. Life has hard knocks

Should I report this attempt of stealth
Or leave him there in lonesome death
I found the photo and hit delete
And with his wife, got something to eat

Taking a Bite of America

I want to sink my teeth into you America,
but I don't know that you still taste right
Your breath blows of dirt and carbon.
Your tongue is swollen with hate.
You've stopped going to school and your flesh hints at stagnation.
Your mottled scalp sheds the hair of idealism.
You stink of animosity.

Your stomach fills with fatalism,
your bowels with the detritus of war
Your skin is pinking up with the cancers of disunion,
the herpes of corruption
Your pockets are emptying of thought and idealism,
your glasses are broken
Your heart is distended with lack of trust,
your skin reeks of dead fish.

What year was it … 1969 …
when you placed your foot on the moon?
When Reverend King had shown us a peaceful way to love?
You seemed to have the taste then of hope and progress.
Now your breath is bad.
If I squeeze you close America will you hug me back?
Or will you bleed out?

Are you still able to make choices by yourself, my fine land?
Or do you need a straightjacket?
Are your sane leaders still in the saddle
 or have they been bucked off by self-interest?
America, I beseech you to start feeding yourself
with the right things.

Like the fruits of labor or the meats of truth.
Spoon into yourself the soup of soul.

You are no longer pregnant with altruism,
or ripe with truth and wisdom
You've closed your arms to those with other-toned skin,
with faiths not in your book
Your skin no longer glows with tolerance.
Your book of wisdom is gone from your pocket.
America, I want to taste you again, to smell your prospects,
to touch your essence

I fear your body is already being grilled up with the fires of greed
I sense your patience is gone for civility,
your time for gentility is faded
There is a dark place just down the road.
It stinks of flesh-eating monsters
I want to taste you once more, America,
but maybe you are over-cooked.

When Our Wings Fall Off

Someone said if they must face their own last day on Earth,
they'd wish to die while doing something they loved the best.
Someone else said their best demise would be while having sex,
another claimed a sunset's glow might start her eternal rest.

My brother Don, a man of flight,
had piloted his whole career.
From B52's, to F-4 ace, to aerobatic flings,
he'd fought aloft in wartime and had stayed aloft in peace.

For me I've not decided which gainful last breath to take.
It could be watching sunsets or seeing grandkids thrive
But reality and statistics say I'll go with a drool in sleep,
or in a stroke-caused fall, or a decrepit heart's last beat.

But brother Don one day, after five decades of flying high,
was in his stunt plane soaring blue upon a Texas sky.
When suddenly a wing came off, he plummeted …
there was no time for plans.
Without regrets it ended …
Don died doing what he loved the most.

Well known in aviation circles,
his eulogy was read by an astronaut
His family grieved; the crowd was huge … war hero laid to rest.
And as we friends and brothers, eyes glistening,
held each other up,
we caught each other's glance and knew: this ending was the best.

As kids we know we'll never die and some of us survive a war,
but later on our wisdom finds no real detour from death

And once resigned to inevitable demise, we blink and then create
the hope that in some way real dignity will hold our hand.

And it's fine to dream orgasmic ends or denouement in glory.
But we should treat our lives as one long flight,
staying high over the clouds of woe.
And the one sure way to have peace is to cherish life
and love and love some more.
So when one day our wings fall off, most likely not in glory,
we pray someone might just stand up and clear their throat …
and with some heartfelt anecdotes …
reward us with our own story.

Struggling to Usurp Nature

Would it were that we controlled the natural world
That man took the helm of nature to have it all unfold
That Neptune and Zeus had loaned us all their powers
To have dominion over seas, the insects and the flowers

We took up with old testaments to pretend we had made it
joined a revolution to let industry rust out the planet
We beefed it up with science; took riches from our core
We copulated, populated, emigrated, more

We bored and drilled, we made motors and smelted
We sawed and we plowed, we shat and we melted
We thought water was endless, that the air would just re-pure
We let money run the rules, somewhere there'd be a cure

We changed the upper air and fogged the lower waters
We tread on space and cured the ills that took away our fathers
We thought we'd supplemented God's Eden with chemical
enhancements
We thought our sphere was faring well, what with man's
achievements

All but a few believed that nature heals itself
Or that some Providence would put danger on the shelf
So somehow it snuck up on us, that some things weren't correcting
We'd overcooked our biosphere, which leaders weren't respecting

Some of us are still asleep, in dreams of earth eternal
Why sacrifice our comforts with fears of an inferno?
Just put more money in the holes that are eroding
We have Dominion, don't we? The Bible tells us so.

We shan't deny our fairways, our highways to the spas
Our gleaming rides, our soaring homes, our sprinkling of the world
And besides, we're told it's just a theory, this place is doing fine
Why just in the last hour, I saw grapes upon the vine.

Look What You Left Me With

How could you have left me like this?
The disease was said to be in remission.
It was so late when they said something was amiss.
We never completed our mission.
I look about for someone to replace you.
I plead at the mirror and you're not there.
I can't sleep in our bed, can't think of someone new.
Tomorrow is just not fair.
I left your shampoo in the shower, your toothbrush in its place.
Our photo has too much power,
I can't move it to make more space.

I remember a night on the shore,
when we both blew kisses at the moon
Can't remember why anymore.
All the reasons will blow away soon.
That faded pink t-shirt you wore 'round the place.
Fuzzy slippers under the bed.
The treasure of that smile on your face.
The plans we made of things ahead.
The way you couldn't back the car.
The way you straightened my tie.
The night you discovered the North Star.
The stealthy way you touched my thigh.

How each of your laughs started with a grunt.
The way you wrote my name.
The fly in the curtains you made me hunt.
The way I took the blame.
You made me stop the car at artsy stores.
You made me swallow up your grace.
You talked me into washing floors.

You feigned that you enjoyed my face.
You always made me rub your feet, while I pretended it was a task.
Doing things for you was easy and you were never afraid to ask.

Now I can't finish things, can't initiate.
Just what can I do for you now, I ask?
How could you let me bear this cross?
I can't lift it, didn't earn it. It's too late.
In the forebodings of my loneliness, the ceiling is my enemy
The bed is my slate of emptiness, your chair a covered memory.
As you left, you gripped my arm
and I still stare at that spot on my skin
You asked me to keep you from harm.
That I couldn't help is my deepest sin.

You never mentioned eternity,
we didn't talk of meeting somewhere later
Our lives were built on certainty, we didn't need a vindicator.
This morning I woke from a dream so sweet.
You had appeared and touched my arm.
You asked if I might rub your feet.
There couldn't have been more charm.
Alas, like many dreams, it was a tease,
your cherished presence but a myth.
In desperation I fall to my knees. Just look what you left me with.

Damn it, they said it was in remission.
But then it stopped your heartbeat.
If love has a two-way vision, why am I here on a one-way street?
Tonight, my dear, I have but one request.
Please let me dream on longer, so I can rub your heart.

What is Family Anyway

What is a family anyway, you ask,
knowing already how you perceive it,
but wondering if I will somehow deconstruct it.
But before I commit to pedantics, I'll check my dictionary.
'A social unit consisting of parents and their children.'
There, simple enough.

So without bringing in sweet violins and baby coos,
I'll try to do mine justice.
I see Mom's haste turn to a smile as she tucked me in,
treating all of us as special
I see her pride as we stood in church to read
a reluctantly mumbled verse
Or returning dirty from scout camp with oak leaves in our clothes

I see Dad grimace when we weren't polite
but smile when we were generous.
And his apparent vow to never once call us names or curse us.
I remember his hug,
held a bit longer when I boarded a plane in uniform
And a small tear when I tendered over
our first cotton-wrapped child to his lap.

I slept under a white Bates bedspread,
protected by Roy Rogers on the wall
On our knees we always recited the same bedtime prayer,
more for her than Him
Four boys and a girl,
we were generously obnoxious and always in trouble
The worst bedtime words were Dad's
"AM I GOING TO HAVE TO COME UP THERE?"

As much as we bickered,
we were fiercely loyal if someone attacked a sib
As much as I often hated my brother,
I was fast to strike someone who pushed him
But I see all-day roasting beef with green beans,
a dessert pie and a hug
I see a litter of kittens and hear Dad's phony threats
to take them away.

There is so much more to family than this ditty.
At best it greets a newborn child
And at worst, it closes a flowered casket on a done-blooming life.
It celebrates unity, thickens our blood,
and thins the miles and the years apart.
Family rewards tolerance and perpetuates loyalty. It plugs us in.

Build Our Children Good Stairways

Sunny smiles key the day
Smooth young skin in every way
Painless energy, ideas blooming
Look only forward, no end is looming

Bright eyes shine with easy tears
The grandkids seem spotless, I see no fears
Endless movement, optimism flows
Their brains seem big, the future glows

Still green enough to sit our laps
We mourn the day their trust will lapse
They still love learning, they read with thirst
I loathe my generation has made it worse

But on an up, life's but a stairway
I have but one job: to clear the airway
To unencumber and smooth their years
And let them run without our fears

We have no right to transfer guilt
We must quell the qualms on which our lives are built
Carry on sweet children, step up, take jumps
If we construct fine stairways, they'll skip the bumps

A Crow at Noon

At dead noon, a crow's call
draws me to the hot garden
The sun is gauze colored
The trees like sad gnomes crushed by heat

What does the crow see?
I look where it is looking and see only listless bushes
The smart bird sees me and ends the call
Hangs up on me and won't tell me the topic

What stirred the crow's voice?
Was there prey or an enemy? A rival?
He is not sharing but he got me out into the sweltering garden.
So I stand in the bird's service, waiting for more commands.

Hot Summer Day

The heat roils up off the pavement like a burning dervish.
The leaves droop limply, flaccid and unwatched.
Blossoms take on pruneish wrinkles and lose their ardor.
The gray cumulus stall in the sky and abandon their edges.

Seeing any human activity, the sun leers closer as if to curb it.
A torpid dog lies staring at nothing in the dusty shade.
A faded food wrapper stays glued against a fence as if eternal.
The shirts cling, creased to our backs, deepened by wet color.

Hope seems perishable and integrity seems to tarnish.
Dried worms stain sidewalks and iron railings reach up like fire.
All but the children seem to wilt and stare towards the sea.
It seems I can hear the glaciers melt and see birds lose air.

The word "ice," hated in winter, sounds now like a lover's call.
The coolness of night, in winter a loss, is now a kind of haven.
I fear my dear has let the heat drain the roses from her hair.
If I pretend to ignore the sun, it yet finds me and fuels its glare.
Hot summer day.

Should I Tell You a Lie?

Should I lie to you with my words to impress you
or to make you think I'm clever?
Can I pile frills onto my facts to show my depth
or to magnify my poetic endeavor?

Is it treasonous to tell lies to a loved one
in order to hold them closer?
Are lies expected and welcomed, even trusted
to add ballast to make the link rosier?

How vital is exact, naked truth
in a world of fragile feelings?
Is patronizing someone a sin
when their life is now spin-wheeling?

Is complete candor a real value
in a relationship long past its peak?
Is an unfiltered mouth a tribute
in a time that is already weak?

Would we bear false witness to prevent
a desperate man from jumping?
Or trim up his self-image with false futures
and glory, security and fine tidings?

Truth is wonderful. It is essential. We can't lose it.
In government it is the key element of trust.
But in love and domestic conditions
An occasional white lie is a must.

Hey, would I lie to you?

Holding Your Grandchildren:
The Candle Burns Quickly

With the tiniest of hands and roundest of faces, they lure you in,
drawing you close to feel the warmth of their heads,
see the lift of their smiles,
touch the wisps of their hair, enhance your own value
by their dependence.
You are soberly aware of the shortness of their time needing you.
Hold them close: the candle of time burns quickly.

With bright eyes following you they share this new world of yours,
which they deserve the best of but is bestowed to them soiled.
The tiny hands grip your finger and the doll-like feet jump about.
You bring your best and warmest game, your graceful kindness.
Hold them close: the candle of time burns quickly.

A face of purity, a mouth of smiles, the eyes are chocked with trust.
Holding them mines out what is left of your purity;
and you try to pass it to them.
You deign to shore yourself up with their reliance.
You try to absorb some the soft pinkness of them onto yourself.
Hold them close: the candle of time burns quickly.

Before the grandchildren came,
you were unaware there was a hole to fill.
They are the new proof there was some reason you grew their parents.
The love you bequeath them will not be in the genes but soaked up in
the hands of their grandparents.
Look into their eyes, give unabashed approval, stream love at them
even if you reach somewhere for it.
Hold them close: the candle of time burns quickly.

Suns, Flowers, and Me

Summer bends the light rays down
to gather on my neck and knees.
The leaves grow lushly, ardently.
We wait: the birds, myself, the bees.

Dramatic spurts of springtime growth
are nurtured too by wetting skies.
And now the colors procreate,
divide and lure my eager eyes.

There are two suns that fill my days:
The one throws wrinkles at my skin,
while the other sustains our luscious earth,
gives life itself, lets flowers begin.

I peer at petals, stamens, stems.
Would love to join their orgies.
I'd love to fly into their hearts
And shepherd in the bees

I'd partake in symbiosis too.
Approve the pollination.
Rejoice to see the hummingbird
come join the presentation.

Alas, these flowers don't want me
Barging on their effervescence.
Perhaps the sun will let me watch
this marvel from a distance.

Why, I could argue that they owe me some.
I throw water in and plant food at their feet.
I photograph them proudly and prune their tired leaves
But if I didn't do it here, they'd find some swale's retreat.

And there without my hovering, they'd pick the sun that's right
And do their daily performances with just the birds in sight.

Can I Touch Him?

Mom and I kneeled in front of the casket, which held Grandpa in a box with way too much satin. His face had been powdered with something; his hair combed all wrong. And they'd jammed him into a tweed suit. I hadn't seen him in a suit. It looked way too stiff. And Grandpa wasn't grinning. He'd always grinned. The funeral home guys must not have known him. He was so much smaller here, and why'd they made his lips so thin?

Mom was saying a prayer, so I tried one too, but it wasn't much. We were surrounded by tons of smelly flowers. Somewhere a speaker was playing an organ song. Grandpa had an old pump organ and they said he played it well, before he went mostly blind. I never knew him then when he could still see, but I did pump away on that organ some and he didn't seem to mind. I was aware of the people behind me watching. My Dad, my cousins, the stiff people from the church.

At first Grandpa seemed plastic but I began to zone in on him and he seemed now warmer. It really was him. I leaned to Mom and said, *"Can I touch Him?"*

"No!" she said. *"You can't touch him. Of course not. That isn't right."*

"Mom, I want to touch Grandpa's face just for a minute. I won't hurt him. And I want to give him this."

"Absolutely not," she declared. *"Let's get up now and let other people in here. Come on."*

After we greeted some neighbors, I drew her into a small fancy sitting room with laced doilies.

"Mom, why didn't you let me touch Grandpa?"

"Now you listen to me," she said. *"It isn't proper."*

She was always a bit too much into propriety and manners. I was not always into them.

She began to describe some of the formalities of funeral visitations, and I started to cry.

61

"And what was that dirty thing you wanted to put in there? You can't just put your stuff in a casket. You're eleven now and need to act like an adult."

"Will you let me say what I want to say, Mom, and don't interrupt me." She stopped and looked at me.

"Mom, the reason I wanted to touch Grandpa is because he always touched me."

"What?" she said. *"Where did he touch you?"*

"No is wasn't that, Mom. Will you listen to me?" I was still crying a little and had my back to the door where aunts and church ladies and stuff were passing by, looking in.

"Okay. You know he couldn't see hardly anything so when we went for walks, he'd stop me and ask if he could touch me. At first I didn't like it but he touched my face while I talked.

A lot of times he held my hands and he felt my arm muscles once. It was okay, Mom.

He wanted know what I felt like, not just what I sounded like, or smelled like, or acted like.

When he took me fishing at Smithson's Dock, he could check by feel how I tied the lure on.

He could tell what kind fish I had on just by the pull. He could take the fish off the hook for me.

When a duck splashed in nearby, Grandpa would ask me what color, then tell me the kind of duck it was.

Mom started to talk, and I held my hand up.

"One day I lost my lure to a snag and I thought my day was over, but Grandpa said, "No. Reach into my tacklebox there and hand me the little scratched lure. It's green and white."

"I did, and without seeing it, he expertly tied it on my line. A minute later I had my best bluegill ever! And Grandpa touched my face and held my shoulders, just to know my joy. It was cool."

Mom interrupted, *"I don't get the point, son. We have to go back into the room. I saw Aunt Mary arrive."*

"Please Mom," I said, holding her to her chair. I created some more tears. *"You see, he touched me because that's part of how he knew me. Now, I want to touch him as my goodbye. I gotta do this, Mom."*

She looked at me, this time with some attention. "I get it now," she said, *"I'm sorry. I'm so caught up in this. Understand that he was your grandpa, but he was my Dad, too."* She put a kleenex to her eye.

She looked at me closely for a minute. *"Let's go back in there and you can go back to the casket."*

We did that, and I touched Grandpa's face and his hands. Then next to me, Mom and Dad kneeled in.

And she touched him too. For quite a while. And I took the old lure from my pocket and put it next to his hands.

A bit later my sister hissed to me, *"Why did you put that ugly fishing thing on his hands?"*

And I gave her a pissy look and said, *"That's for me to know and you to find out."*

And the organ played.

The Spy on Rue Malchance

The gray stone street sits heavy in the rainy Parisian night.
The aging spy pretends to read his paper under a dim streetlight.
Two SS soldiers skip loudly by, tugging a giggling salon girl.
They don't notice the spy in his trench coat,
or that he begins to follow.
The drunken trio stops in front of a closed fromagerie.
They pretend to break the window and to steal a cheese,
then stagger on.

The spy trods on, his wide chapeau stopping the rain.
He hesitates whenever they do, and then splashes on.
The girl reaches towards their pants, then dashes ahead in laughter.
One of the men slips and falls and they all dance about it
in the reflecting puddles.
A brown Renault taxi hurries by, annoying the puddles
and glancing them aside.
A wine bottle flies from the taxi and the soldiers pretend anger;
their fists high.

The spy's wife, Colette, had been warm and serene,
her love for him clear and straight.
Her letter, condemning the German occupation of the city,
had appeared in *Les Temps*.
The Gestapo came one day and took her away.
The desperate spy inquired everywhere.
The Provisiore Police had no answers. Breaking rules,
he sent a desperate note to his superior.
In two days: a note under his door.
Colette's body had been found in an alley.
Just off Rue Malchance. Her eyes had been cut out;
her writing hand cut off.

The rain does not let up as the trio frisks their way
along Rue Malchance.
They enter an apartment building while the spy lingers,
away from a streetlamp.
The spy lights a Gitane and waits.
A window lights brightly on the second floor.
After a time, he enters the foyer and slips off
his wet souliers to quiet his ascent.
He checks his Beretta and pulls out the surgical scalpels.
He climbs the stair.
The door is not locked.
He kicks it open and says, *"Ceci, pour Colette!"* He enters.

Blood Flow. Life Flow

How did they slip past me, those things I remember?
The gauzy tired walks to the stairway to go to bed,
tugged in my mother's hand
Her hands then smooth and firm but later the skin pulled inwards
and convoluted into colored rivers and valleys of translucent skin,
and the years after she died also turned into veins and hollows.
Our life flow might have parallels to our cardiovascular flow.
Fresh and young it leaves our vibrant hearts
and finds its arterial way out to our hopeful lives.
Then spent, it returns veinously without its oxygen,
seeking a rebirth from its vital hub.
But gradually with age, each time now it goes out less far,
and returns to its heartthrob less rich
So the next lifeblood trip cannot reach
the places its path to our wishes' desires.
What stood in the way of all that sunshine?
Who parched and defoliated our hopes?
We ran, now we walk. We climbed, now we but trod.
We rose, but now we hang on.
The path to the sun has darkened
and the golden stairway is beyond our reach.
We were hatchlings, perched on the edge to fly.
Now we look longingly towards the nest.
Our petals and stamens were the lure for our young.
Now they look for fresher blooms.
We stand here in our rumpled years, tossing blossoms out
and watching them fall short
The stars no longer fall into our hands, the rainbows are pale,
and fewer seek our counsel
Someone bright and lush spots us and rushes towards us.
New hope, enhanced circulation.

We reach to embrace them, but they fly right past us
to better waters, stronger heartflow.
I reached to pick up a newborn, but by the time it was in my arms,
it had grown old.

How did they all slip past me?

Next Bus to Korea

I see a boy at the Greyhound station.
He is nine and it is 1951. He is watching the soldiers boarding
Bound for the coast, then to Korea.
Flint's young men, black and white
Rich and poor, but all their pants are pressed equally,
their shoes gleam, the brass is straight

They hug their mothers, lips quivering, acting cavalier.
The bus is rounded, jet-like, with chrome details
and its diesel looms in a worldly way.
The boy is intrigued, wondering how many commies they'll shoot.
He wonders if they'll see MacArthur in person on the front.

The loudspeaker's words drew the men more rapidly up the steps
On their way to heroism and destiny
and the newsreels at the Gem Theater
Just a few years back in the last war,
the boy's good friend Jim had told him
About his father, who didn't come home from Italy, but not why.
He was afraid to ask.

But his other friend Dave's Dad had died in a jeep wreck near Rome.
And now only half a decade later in Korea,
his friend Mike's uncle had just died at Heartbreak Ridge.
And his cousin Billy was right now near the "Reservoir,"
whatever that was.
He wondered if these gallant bus-boarding men,
so tall and straight would go protect Billy.

And let him come home to his mother, Aunt Mary.
John Wayne always came home.
The boy and a black kid about the same age,
exchanged glances, like 9-year-olds do
The kid said, "That's my Daddy,"
and pointed proudly to some bus window

He wondered if black soldiers died any easier than white soldiers,
or any harder.

The bus vroomed loudly and fumed its way out and into a night rain
The kid asked him, "Is your Daddy on the bus too?"
"No" he said. "My sister is coming in from college. Next bus."
"Oh," said the kid. "That's nice. Is your Daddy a soldier?"
"No." said the boy. "He's too old." "Oh," said the kid. "You're lucky."

The squawky speaker changed to Nat King Cole singing "Mona Lisa."
A fresh wet bus pulled under the lights, soon dripping off its passengers
My sister clutched my mother but briefly, a college girl now
And she grinned at some of the soldiers forming a line
for the next bus out for Korea.

You Think That Was a Storm?

So, you think that was a storm?
I'll tell you about real storms.
I'm older now; have earned the right to stimulate the truth.
With your permission I'll let you in, on storms of greater stuff.

The snows came then for days on end
We'd see no others for weeks.
We melted snow for drinking,
And killed our lamb for food.

The trees broke down and travelers died
The cows froze on their feet
We huddled close and shared the blankets
And new babies showed up next fall

We ran out of firewood,
then fueled the stove with Grandpa's library
Aunt Mary's chifforobe burned next, then mother's cedar chest
We trekked out to old Bossy and milked her down
But all we got was ice cream.

And then one day the sun emerged
We crawled, coinless, to the store
We traded in old Bart the pig
For bread flour, oatmeal and more

So, don't tell me about yesterday's storm
which only shut the school
Or you'll have to hear of our great storms we had with one another
Like the bitter one at Donner Pass that lasted many weeks
And after starving half to death, we dined upon each other.

Now THAT'S a storm, and tasty too: young Ned was our dessert
So, when we need to curb our population,
let's have a Donner Storm.
I'll bring the mittens and silverware,
You bring the wine and condiments.

What Have I Learned?

That watching a puppy run into a chair leg is a perfect learning lesson.
I have learned that there are no lasting rewards for winning arguments.
That your neighbor's barbecuing smells better than yours.
That a child is never cold when trying out their new bike
on Christmas morning.
That as you age you get more interested in humans than money.
That one of the best fitness exercises I can do is to thicken my skin.
That life's rewards have more to do with how you act
than what you believe.
That language grows wisdom, and wisdom grows language.
That receiving a handwritten thank-you note is better.
That the connection between knowledge and tolerance is real.
That walking down a trail is great, but blazing a new trail is greater.
That a newly-opened pizza box is almost better than sex.
That we never get tired or rainbows and sunsets.
That in marriage, compromise pays back way better than victories.
That if you wash the dishes with someone you really like, it is fun.
That I before I exercise, I often forget how good I feel after.
That spotting yourself in a store mirror and finding it okay, is a reward.
That I will always pay a grandchild to scratch my head.
That finding out a friend loves the same song you do, is a treasure.
That watching the steam on your coffee cup
is sometimes the best you can do.
That the smarter people I know can address ideas, not just people.
That placing an extra blanket on a child at bedtime is always rewarding.
That there is mac & cheese. And then there is MAC & CHEESE!
That the best resolutions are not about what you eat,
but how you treat others.
That waking up to pee and then actually going back to sleep is a miracle.
That we might have to set aside some greed to save humanity.
That Yogi Berra was right when he said:
"When you come to a fork in the road, take it."
That I missed every shot I didn't take.

73

George Wylie is a former office worker and former history instructor at a Michigan college. A graduate of the University of Michigan, he lives with his wife Rita in Southeastern Michigan, after living many years on a Northern lake. They have two grown sons and five grandchildren. Among his many interests, George counts poetry, gardening, photography, humor writing, bicycling, kayaking, grand parenting, politics, and travel as his favorites. With only three years of writing poetry, George's pieces have appeared in three anthologies, Allpoetry.com, and several poetry contests. This is his first book. For the spoken word, George often visits the online World Poetry Open Mic. He hosts a Facebook poetry page called George Wylie Writes, is a co-leader of the Downriver Poets & Playwrights group and is a member of the Poetry Societies of Michigan and Indiana. Should you wish to contact George, his email is: ghwylie@gmail.com

Made in the USA
Lexington, KY
11 September 2019